For Don, Peter, Sara and Joanna
M.M.L.

To the Woodworms, and to Silke
D.P.

Published by The Millbrook Press, Inc.
2 Old New Milford Road
Brookfield, CT   06804
www.millbrookpress.com

Text copyright © 2001 by Michelle
Myers Lackner
Illustrations copyright © 2001 by
Daniel Powers
Printed in Hong Kong
Library of Congress Cataloging-in-
Publication Data
Lackner, Michelle Myers.
Toil in the soil / Michelle Myers Lackner;
illustrated by Daniel Powers.
p.   cm.
ISBN 0-7613-1807-0 (lib. bdg.)
1. Earthworms—Juvenile literature.
[1. Earthworms.] l. Powers, Daniel, ill.
II. title.
QL391.A6 L327 2001
592'.64—dc21   00-036150

Toil in the Soil

MICHELLE MYERS LACKNER

ILLUSTRATIONS BY

DANIEL POWERS

THE MILLBROOK PRESS
Brookfield, Connecticut

Chew, toss, tear,

splatter, smash, squish,

munch, crunch, fight!

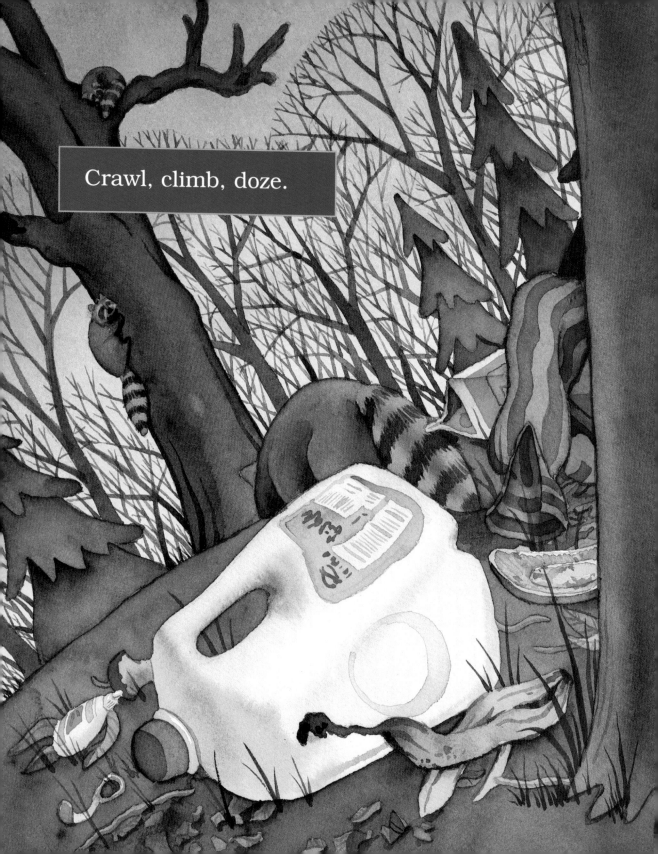

Crawl, climb, doze.

Work, worms, work.

Tumble, scatter, crumble.

Grab, worms, grab.

Wind blows, roots tear, tree crashes;

Tug, worms, tug.

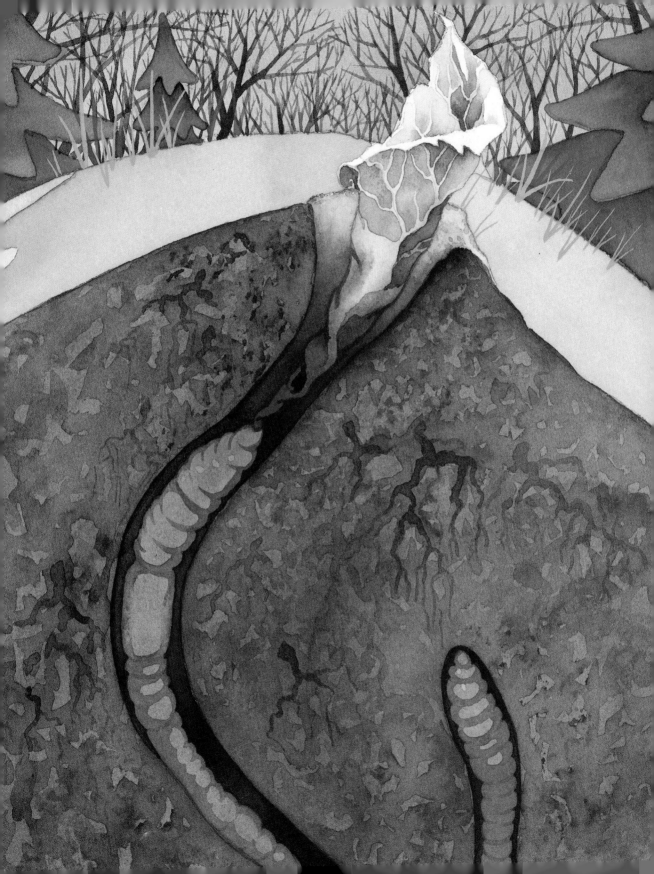

Lightning strikes, wood
sparks, fire blazes!

Tunnel, worms, tunnel!

Snow falls, ice grips, forest sleeps;

Wait, worms, wait.

Rain pelts, snow melts, burrows fill;

S-t-r-e-t-c-h, worms, s-t-r-e-t-c-h.

Sun shines, earth
warms, robin spies;

Hide, worms, hide!

Fungus grows, mites munch, bark rots;

Nibble, worms, nibble.

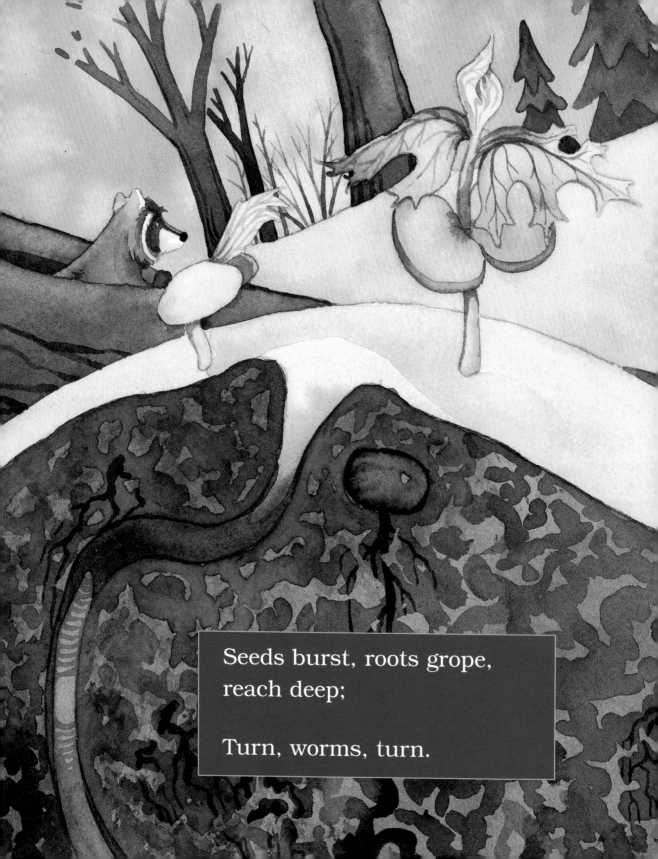

Seeds burst, roots grope, reach deep;

Turn, worms, turn.

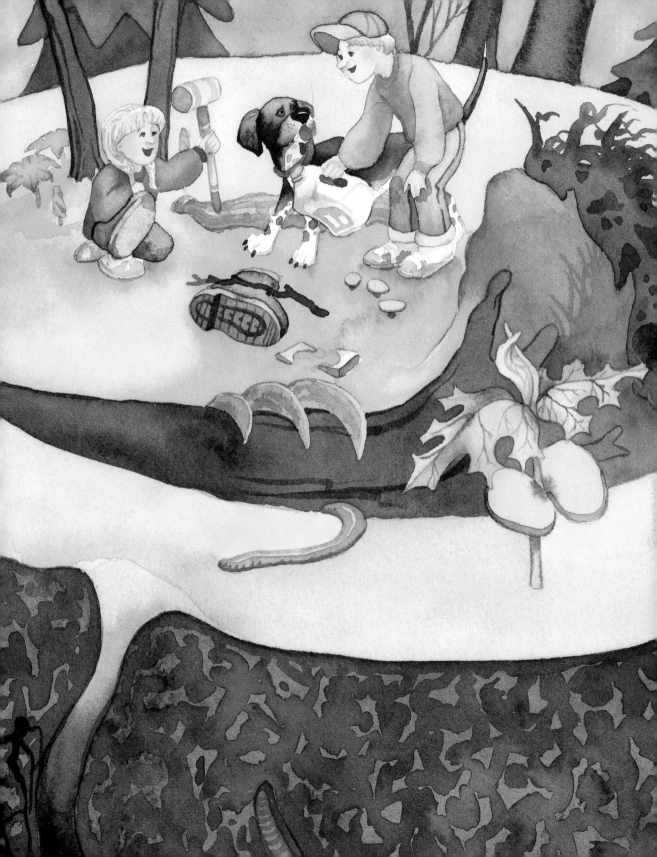

Seasons pass, flowers bloom, trees tower . . .

. . . and tumble. Everything returns to earth.

Toil, worms, toil.

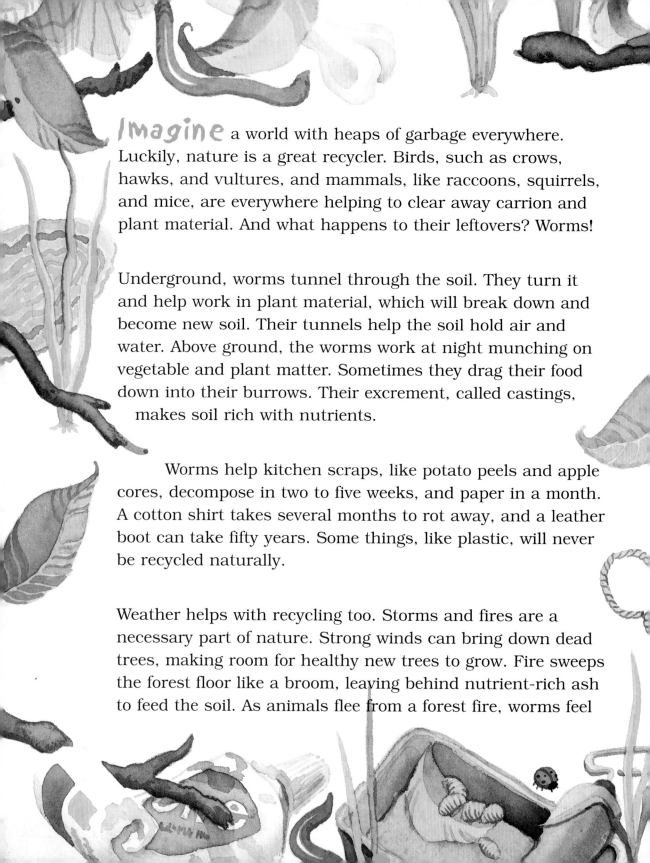

Imagine a world with heaps of garbage everywhere. Luckily, nature is a great recycler. Birds, such as crows, hawks, and vultures, and mammals, like raccoons, squirrels, and mice, are everywhere helping to clear away carrion and plant material. And what happens to their leftovers? Worms!

Underground, worms tunnel through the soil. They turn it and help work in plant material, which will break down and become new soil. Their tunnels help the soil hold air and water. Above ground, the worms work at night munching on vegetable and plant matter. Sometimes they drag their food down into their burrows. Their excrement, called castings, makes soil rich with nutrients.

Worms help kitchen scraps, like potato peels and apple cores, decompose in two to five weeks, and paper in a month. A cotton shirt takes several months to rot away, and a leather boot can take fifty years. Some things, like plastic, will never be recycled naturally.

Weather helps with recycling too. Storms and fires are a necessary part of nature. Strong winds can bring down dead trees, making room for healthy new trees to grow. Fire sweeps the forest floor like a broom, leaving behind nutrient-rich ash to feed the soil. As animals flee from a forest fire, worms feel

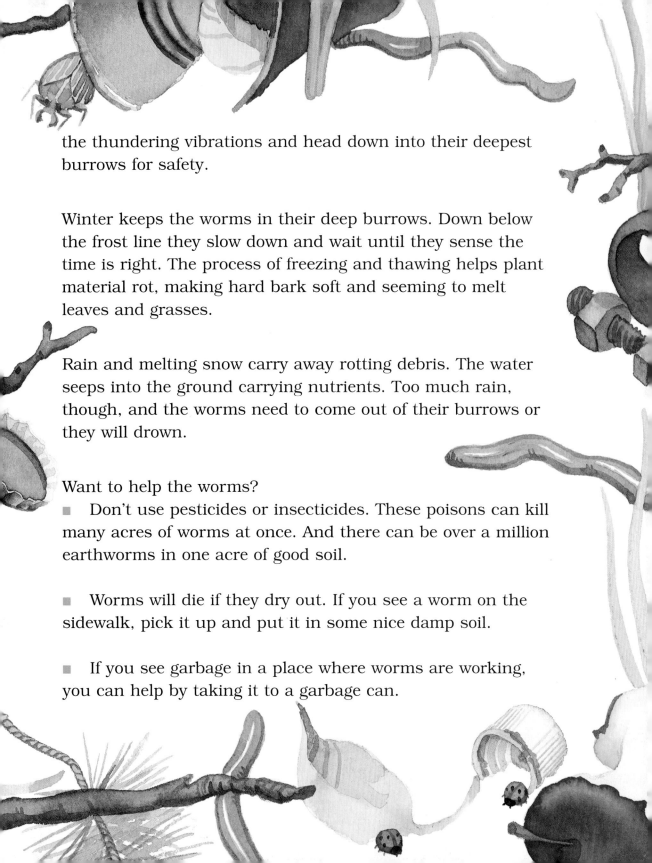

the thundering vibrations and head down into their deepest burrows for safety.

Winter keeps the worms in their deep burrows. Down below the frost line they slow down and wait until they sense the time is right. The process of freezing and thawing helps plant material rot, making hard bark soft and seeming to melt leaves and grasses.

Rain and melting snow carry away rotting debris. The water seeps into the ground carrying nutrients. Too much rain, though, and the worms need to come out of their burrows or they will drown.

Want to help the worms?

- Don't use pesticides or insecticides. These poisons can kill many acres of worms at once. And there can be over a million earthworms in one acre of good soil.

- Worms will die if they dry out. If you see a worm on the sidewalk, pick it up and put it in some nice damp soil.

- If you see garbage in a place where worms are working, you can help by taking it to a garbage can.

About the Author

Michelle Myers Lackner lives in Minnesota with her husband, three children, two cats, a dog, and several worm-rich gardens. She keeps a phenology journal, noting changes in the weather or when plants come into bloom or when the geese fly overhead. Michelle thinks the life of a worm is a bit like the life of a writer —endless toiling for rich rewards!

About the Illustrator

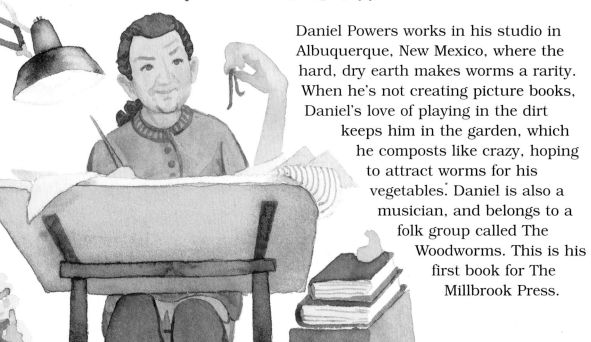

Daniel Powers works in his studio in Albuquerque, New Mexico, where the hard, dry earth makes worms a rarity. When he's not creating picture books, Daniel's love of playing in the dirt keeps him in the garden, which he composts like crazy, hoping to attract worms for his vegetables. Daniel is also a musician, and belongs to a folk group called The Woodworms. This is his first book for The Millbrook Press.